Ink Of

Kasturi Datta

Ink Of A Dreamer © 2022 Kasturi Datta

All rights reserved.

No part of this publication may be reproduced, stored in a retrieval system, or transmitted, in any form or by any means, electronic, mechanical, photocopying, recording or otherwise, without the prior written permission of the presenters.

Kasturi Datta asserts the moral right to be identified as author of this work.

Presentation by *BookLeaf Publishing*

Web: www.bookleafpub.com

E-mail: info@bookleafpub.com

ISBN: 9789357617369

First edition 2022

This book for anybody who opens it...loved one and strangers alike!

ACKNOWLEDGEMENT

This book would not have been possible without my mamma, her support and patience while reading through a million drafts. Thank you to my papa and brother who have shown excitement from the very beginning of this journey and have continued to support me throughout.

And a thank you to the people in my life who have inspired some of the poems in this book, even though they are not aware of it!

Melody of Time

One note after the other,
the clockwork of a melody had begun.
Wine-tainted conversation stopped
mid-syllable,
any person who spoke would be held
culpable
of awakening the Time monster.

It preyed.
On those sustained by the
breath in-between beats of the music,
those who could step beyond its reach
and ascend
like the voice of a violin,
leaving the bass of reality behind.

All that was beautiful he
had frozen.
Standstill gazes of awe
and the only movement were his fingers,
the pianist kept hearts in suspension
note after note,
as he played the melody of time.

Twilight Waltz

Sunset colours swam
in the martini,
sinking lower & lower
but the glass remained full.

Gentlemen coaxed in Givenchy &
words dripping with ego and whiskey,
trying harder & harder
but her head did not turn.

Dusk began to bleed &
the darkening sky set her nerves alight,
red lipstick marked the glass
as she began her love affair with the night.

Moonlight flooded in through the
window of her backless dress,
the stars asked her for a dance,

& they waltzed
to the cries of the dying sunset.

Flowers and Glass

Born into a fleshy prison, she was
compared to a white rose before
having any real substance to bloom.

Beauty followed her like cameras
followed Marilyn Monroe.

"Pretty" and "gorgeous" made up
her entourage and "thank you" hid the
avalanche of anxiety, mixed with voices of
women they thought she would outgrow.

But truth was not a phase like
bleached blue hair.

Her spotlight was meant for more
than showing off her contour on untouched skin
and
curves available for purchase

by girls trying to fill empty frames, being told to
try and look like her one day.

Shackled by definitions of femininity, yet
she learnt to fly and break

glass ceilings

with the weight of the words tied to her ankles:
"Act like a woman".

So, she cleaned and gathered the
shards of glass, some showed her
tears and some held her fear that to make them
listen,

she would have to make them bleed.
But it was her blood they wanted

to use as ink for her to sign
the contract of womanhood, but instead
she bled when she planted the shards of glass

in a garden.
So the next flower to bloom
will not be called "pretty",

but be known for growing despite carrying
pieces of the enemy in its veins.

A Choice

If words shone like diamonds,
would you wear them proudly across your neck?
Or leave them in neglect,
to gather dust in a box
inside your throat?

If words burnt like oil,
would you play with them blindly
near an open flame?
Would you watch as the embers of your fire
scar those you never wanted in harm's way.

If words aged like wine
getting stronger over time,
would you pause before planting the seeds
and nurture the growth of the vine?
Or sow with recklessness,

risking the burn of the bitter aftertaste that will
follow
words you planted long ago.

Conversations With Myself

Conversations with myself
are some of the best I've ever had,
speaking in tongues of gibberish and fiction
without neither thinking the other is mad.

Conversations with myself
are some of the funniest I've ever had,
recounting embarrassment, nostalgia and
growing from the moments where it all went
bad.

Conversations with myself
are some of the most honest I've ever had,
no room for judgements or expectations
but a remedy of truth for when I feel sad.

Conversations with ourselves
are sometimes just what we need,
although it may seem daunting
to confront
things easily hidden by friends
and drinks,
hearing the words you've known along
will help you to be free.

Grandmother

I opened my grandmother's diary
and a strip of negatives fell to the floor,
moments of her life, captured by the light
in the palm of my hand.
It made me smile, to imagine my grandmother through
the lens of a camera, no desire for posing
or looking the photographer in the eye
to say "cheese".
She preferred to be the artist, having control over the darkness
of a person's outline,
mastery over the blending of inks.
The steadiness of her hand is forever held in the
stare of the faces that she has drawn. People immortalised
by her paintbrush in a life where she has known
them to be temporary.

The diary was written in the language of the land
where my mother was born, the shapes
made of ink were foreign to me. But the negatives
showed me the writer,

an orphan- who could have blended away into grey-
a few years shy of becoming the woman who smiles at me now
from an oak frame on my window.
In difficult times I think of my grandmother, wrapped up in her nineties,
sending and receiving kisses on the phone.
Of the choice she made to change
shades of loneliness into love. She is an artist, and the grandest masterpiece she ever painted is her life.

In The Fall

Tree leaves dipped in golden
orange and red honey, makes a forest
in Autumn such a sweet sight for eyes,

sweet like delicious sips of Pumpkin Spice
in a crowded café, one that is filled with
chilled hands and woollen scarves,

bodies wrapped warm but hearts are exposed,
hanging onto the sleeves of
Autumn-lovers who walk along the forest
ground
covered in honey-dipped leaves,
crunch,
       crunch,
              crunch
goes the song of Fall,
playing as nature falls in the thrall of change
and her surrender is a beautiful sight to behold.

Love in the Universe

Kisses from the ocean are carried
in shapeless puffballs across a blue atmosphere.

Or is it pink?

We may never know, just as
Sun and Moon are yet to know each other
beneath the surface of their glow, but when one takes
to the stage the other falls out of sight.

The same cannot be said for Thunder
who chases lightning like a hopeless romantic,
their lover's quarrel bringing the sky to life
while people look up from below

in awe, of how the chase between their mind and heart
is reflected in the heavens above.

The Devil Wept

The Devil prays
and Angels steal rewards for themselves
when confessional halls are empty.
Disappearing into the abyss
behind closed eyes
is where the Devil can hide for a moment,
as hollow souls
ring the bell outside.

Shadows at his command and
demons sat in wait under thumb
all sing chords of pain,
notes of helplessness and anger reverberate,
through the walls to the metronome of regret
that these souls were not descended upon
before inhuman deeds were done.

The Devil weeps as the bell rings out
for centuries,
Angels laugh at him from the other side,
throwing broken halos as confetti to celebrate
the monster who cried
like the men, women, and children on earth
who begged for mercy.

Fluffy Friends

The gift of eternal friendship
comes with a wagging tale,
from the first drop of sunrise
and all through the night they think
of you,

-and maybe treat or two -

with the biggest of smiles
in their eyes,
the boldest exclamations of love
in their jumps, belly rubs
and being told they're oh-so good,

-but they know that already from
all the extra food-

their loyalty stuffs our hearts
and keeps us full of wonder
at how we can be taught so much,
by the silence of words and
the noise of innocence,

theirs is a simple existence,
with the purpose of adding more love
to a world filled with people searching,
for the promise of an unconditional bond.

Every Now And Then

When do I stop missing you?...
...The front cover has changed but the story
remains the same. No longer do I mix my cereal
with denial or tears with my tea, but I still get a
taste.
Every now and then
of something that slipped out of my hand
but not out of my mind.
It feeds the illusion that I have not
moved on, but
every day I move,
further from the photograph of happiness and
closer to the negatives of the truth,
that we were always meant to be
something to stay as a memory.

Rubik's Cube

Place a completed Rubik's Cube
in front of me,
but do not expect me to marvel
at its beauty,
I would rather praise the chaos
that came before.

A single green on the face
of eight reds paints an image
of perfection within reach,
but the single imperfection is what
keeps the journey alive.

A cube paused in rotation is all
that is needed to make diamonds appear,
an irregularity with shape-shifting edges
can only mean that insanity is near.

Ever-changing colours and
three-sixty degree turns
until you question why you ever started
this endless pursuit,

excitement turns into resentment
as hours pass, but

the colourful succession of
trials and errors is the
ultimate puzzler's trophy.

Snowflakes

I often find myself awake, while the
rest of the street sleeps,
my imagination creeps out of the closed window
and hovers under the glow of the yellow
lamplight.

Free-falling particles of snow show
me a fantasy, each one is a piece
from my memory of Christmases
long ago,
new snow falling upon old ground
like children planting kisses
on grandad and grandma's nose.

Nostalgia and happiness yet to unfold
are the snowflakes that I see
under the lamplight glow,
a little after midnight,
while the rest of the street sleeps.

Hero

I've heard the words,
'you are your own hero', held
them closely to other truths that have been
written in lost and found diaries,
but when I was my own enemy
I prayed for the words to transform
into hands,
to dry my tears and hold up stop signs
for the strangers running amok in my head.

Picking new locations but
but finding my feet stood on ground
at the same destination,
this was my fate,
an addiction to self-doubt was the
direction I could not escape,
but one day I looked behind,
to see that all the roads
I travelled down were different,
and suddenly the destination
had changed.

Memory of the light inside has
been my saving grace,
but memory also takes me back

to that time
when the mess seemed too big to be
cleaned up by other truths,
sometimes I feel afraid that the strangers will
try to reclaim
my mind, their property.

But then I just take a breath
and remember,
that a Hero has already made a
home in there.

To Love A Writer

It is not simple to love a writer,
For they are many people with the same face,
At breakfast you could be sat next to a hopeless romantic,
Come dinnertime and she is a criminal awaiting a chase.

She does not need protection from the world,
Because she has weapons aplenty,
Ink loaded with truth, sharp words under the guise of red lips,
Her arsenal is never empty.

If you buy her diamonds,
She will swap them for ancient treasure from an unknown land,
Bring her flowers,
And she will walk you through a technicolour rainforest while
you hold them in your hand.

To love her will be difficult,
But also one of the best things you could do,
Because she can create entire worlds and souls of her own design,
And she has chosen to love you.

Where Has All The Ice Gone?

New hearts start to beat,
the ice keeps melting,
because of all those who came before
and the trades made between nature and mankind.
Only one side had more to gain.

Eager believers with milk teeth and without sleep
await Santa and sleigh bells,
imagining his home in its magnificent snow-clad glory.
Meanwhile the polar bear scrambles for floating chunks of ice.

Fridge magnets of our friends with beaks, flippers,
the ones with big teeth and the ones with fur,
are living on land they think will last forever,
but disappearing icebergs do little to keep mother
bear's worries at bay.
The water keeps on rising.

Change is flowing through the veins
of earth and
poisoning the blood of her history,
the damage cannot be reversed,
controlling what falls in its path is the only
remedy,
before time has melted all ice and
we are left with frozen hearts.

Heart In A Bottle

I wrapped up my heart in a love letter
and sent it across the ocean,

in a glass bottle for all creatures of the
deep to see,

warmed by the sun and cooled by the moonlight
as it floated further away from me,

love is the mightiest of sailors,
no wave or sea storm strong enough to
alter its course,

so, I knew my heart would sail on,
until the glass bottle found itself on some distant
land,

where he who is salvaged by a collection of
fading memories will read my letter,

and know that his footprints in the sand will
remain
for as long as my heart beats in his hands.

I dreamt I was a caterpillar

I dreamt I was a caterpillar,
oblivious of the beautiful creature I would
one day become,
contently eating leaves and being left
to catch up to my faster friends,

but then came the meadow where
they disappeared,
fear grasped tightly onto all eight pairs of my
legs,
blades of grass like mouth-watering skyscrapers
before me,
I was soon to be surrounded by a green haze
but then I changed my gaze
to the sky,

I started to wish that I could fly,
above and across the meadow filled with
colourful
flowers of a condescending height,
safe from larger neighbours of whom I did not
know,

but I remained on the ground
on the other side of the meadow,

contently eating leaves, wishes fading
from my memory.

My dream shifted and I
was powerless as my body peacefully slept,
trapped away in a silk cage, I thought
I had been engulfed by the green haze,

after the unknowing had taken place,
somehow, something had cut open
an escape for me,
I emerged to find raindrops holding an image
of a pair of iridescent wings,
the wind whispered in a language that
was once an untranslatable breeze.

And then I flew,

across the meadow, my ruby wings made
the flowers look up in jealousy
at the caterpillar,
who didn't know what she had done
to make her wish come true.

Miles Away

Teardrops fell and
raindrops raced down the window
of the car that was taking me
further away from you,

driving in the direction of a goodbye
along roads that stretched like
my fingers did for yours
under the blanket,
hidden away from inevitability.

Rear view mirrors taunted me
when I looked at the distance building behind,
because there was no turning
these four wheels back
towards the home where your
fingers had found mine.

Miles away from the smiles
I shared with you,
with only memories stored safely in the trunk
of my mind, confessions archived in my heart
and in my pocket was a love
folded away,
wishing it could go home.

Our Mystery

Mystery and confusion began
with our first breath,
a sudden arrival into a room
with very bright lights,
onto a planet
with a lot of noise.

Walking, crawling,
climbing and falling,
all that is achieved before we can
even count beyond 15, without
getting distracted by
our favourite show on the telly.

Love enters our existence itinerary
without warning,
through the backdoor of a favourite song
or a first kiss,
quite often during a
hug with a dog,

and the confusion grows
when thoughts are kicked out by feelings,
when hands that were once warmed
by another fall empty,

and the painter behind grey skies
is impossible to find.

Yet we arrived into
this mystery
not to make sense of the storm,
but to fall and live like rain,
use grey skies to paint our own rainbows
and help the earth to grow.

My Week

On Monday, you can find me
wrapped in a blanket,
sat on the curve of the crescent moon
trying to roast marshmallows on the flame
of the closest star.

On Tuesday, you can spot me by
the yellow sails of my boat,
an alien in the middle of a school of
dolphins,
with only the North star and waves to guide me.

On Wednesday, you will find me
on the highest branch of a tree,
carving secret messages into wood and
at peace with all that is out of reach below,
hidden by the canopy of leaves.

On Thursday, you need only look
behind and you will find me there
with open arms,
an epiphany or two and
a bag of nachos for us to share.

On Friday, the only place I will be

is in the palm of a giant's hand,
he who sits atop Mt. Everest and sings to
Sinatra,
while I lie aligned with his palm lines
and hum along.

On Saturday, I am hidden away inside
the body of a piano,
hopping between alternating strings and dodging
the fall of the hammers,
vibrations dance beneath my feet as notes are
born.

Then comes Sunday when I cannot be found
on the moon, or up in a tree,
but with my head resting on my mum's shoulder,
the place that has always held
the best view of the world for me.

www.ingramcontent.com/pod-product-compliance
Ingram Content Group UK Ltd.
Pitfield, Milton Keynes, MK11 3LW, UK
UKHW021414240125
4287UKWH00047B/665